Celestial Dynamics;

A COURSE OF

Astro-Metaphysical Study,

BY THE AUTHOR OF

"The Language of the Stars."
AND
"The Light of Egypt"

PUBLISHED BY
THE ASTRO-PHILOSOPHICAL PUBLISHING CO.
DENVER, COLO.
1896.

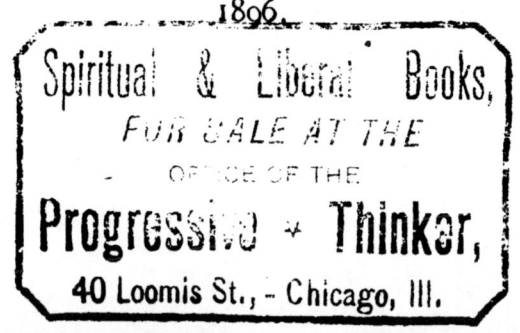

**Kessinger Publishing's Rare Reprints
Thousands of Scarce and Hard-to-Find Books!**

We kindly invite you to view our extensive catalog list at:
http://www.kessinger.net

PREFACE.

"There are more things in heaven and earth, Horatio,
than are dreamt of in your philosophy."—*Shakespeare.*

And there are more powers, forces and entities in nature than metaphysical practitioners and healers have hitherto thought of much less taken into consideration, and the time has come when such forces must be recognized and acted upon; hence this course of study, the object of which is to deal with, and if possible to elucidate these hidden powers. Whether or not we shall succeed in our difficult task remains to be seen.

The following brief explanation of our title will be of advantage: The words "Celestial Dynamics" have been chosen as the broad distinguishing title of that section of human knowledge which would be embraced within a complete science of mental and metaphysical life within embodied conditions; a science devoted almost exclusively to the imponderable elements of the human organism; "Celestial," in the sense of being ethereal, and similar to those heavenly centers from which the activities emanate, and "Dynamics," as applied to actual force *in motion*.

Publishers' Preface.

It was the intention of both the author and publishers to give the reading public "Celestial Dynamics" shortly after the publication of "The Language of the Stars," in 1892, as announced on the cover of that book, but circumstances, over which we have had no control, caused the delay until now. This explanation is thought sufficient apology to all those who have repeatedly asked when "Celestial Dynamics" would be published. The times are more propitious, and the demand much greater for this valuable work to-day than ever before. Therefore its delay will prove its teachings to be true. "There is a time for everything under the sun." The time for "Celestial Dynamics" is *now*. May it ever find those ready for its teachings, prepared to realize its sublime truths so ably stated by its author, whose life motto is "Omnia Vincit Veritas."

INTRODUCTION.

The most advanced scientific opinion of to-day is rapidly nearing the goal of spiritual recognition, and is even now unconsciously dealing with the imponderable principles of Occult law. Prof. Tyndall, in his work upon "Heat," Lecture XII, thus eloquently describes the shining central reservoir of energy, "and as surely as the force which moves the clock's hands is derived from the arm which winds up the clock, so surely *is all* terrestrial power drawn from the sun. * * * Every mechanical action on the earth's surface, every manifestation of power, organic, or inorganic, vital and physical, is produced by the sun. He lifts the rivers and glaciers up to the mountains. * * * Thunder and lightning are also his transmuted strength. * * * The sun comes to us as heat; he quits us as heat; and between his entrance and departure the multiform powers of our globe appear." *They are all special forms of Solar power.* Louis Figuier, the author of "The World Before the Deluge," and many other scientific productions, in one of his latest works, "The To-morrow of Death," thus speculates, "In the Sun, seasons are known are known no more than days. Time seems to have no existence for the dwellers in that glorious home. The changes and succession of things which make up life for us are unknown to their sublime essence. Duration has no measure in that happy world," (Chapter XII).

The foregoing extracts have been given to show the general trend of science regarding the principles which form the immutable foundation upon which Celestial Dynamics is based.

The glorious central sun of our solar system that rays forth his electrical life for the sustenance of his magnificent family of worlds is, in its material expression and law, but the external covering for the grander and more ethereal spiritual sun, which forms the celestial spheres of the Solar Angels, of whose infinite radiance, wisdom and power we can form no just conception, even as the physical body of man upon the earth is but the material covering, upon the third dimensional plane, of the bright indwelling Soul within. "As it is below, so it is above," as on the material earth, even so do we find the same eternal principles in the shining heavens above. Accordingly, when we recognize in the sun as the radiating center of all forms of energy and power, light heat and electricity, all of which are but different modes of motion, *all* the outcome of nature's sympathetic response to that awful and inconceivable center of Deific uibration, we can, at once, comprehend, as did the ancient Seer, the self-evident fact that we owe everything to *Him* the great *Sun God* of science to-day. He is the immediate source of all we possess; our bodies are dependant upon His never-ceasing action; our food and clothing are the generous gifts of His electrical bounty, and our Soul's inspiration and unfoldment are the evolutionary outcome of the same celestial power, for life, light and love are the eternal manifestations of this radiant center.

In our endeavors to understand the hidden workings of nature's law, we must ever bear in mind that the outward form is but the concrete symbol of an interior cause. The physical sun, as the life-giver of earth, exerts the requisite grade of force necessary for the earth's fullest manifestation, while the Spiritual sun, of which the physical orb is the body, exerts the requisite degree of celestial energy, which in *matter* becomes *occult force*, and in man *will and mental power*.

There is sunlight upon the earth radiating all the natural forces required for nature's wondrous unfoldment, and there is an ethereal sunlight streaming from the same center, illuminating with its spiritual rays both the disembodied Soul and the mind of incarnated genius, for the infinite power which gives animal that instinct so akin to reason, to insects their marvelous skill, and to the nightingale its melodious song, is equally with the purer spiritual light of the human Soul in its highest estate, derived from the Deific center of celestial love.

The reader is requested to study closely in connection with this lesson, chapters I, II and III of part II, in "The Light of Egypt." These chapters will clearly explain the distribution of Solar force into planetary influence.

CHAPTER I.

The Occult Forces Of Nature.

What a wondrous creature is man; and what a wondrous universe it is by which he finds himself eternally surrounded. Day by day, ever prompted by the struggling intuitions of the Spirit, science is tearing the grim masks of error and illusion aside, and, night by night, while the weary brain is seeking physical rest, the tireless impulsive Soul is winging its way through the starlit spaces of Aeth, ever and anon making new discoveries, sensing grander systems and universes than its own, vaguely dreaming of yet more awful mysteries slumbering within the evolutionary uterus of time and ever longing and aspiring to quench its insatiable thirst for knowledge in the light, love and truth of that Divine wisdom for which it yearns; but forever unable to reach the ideal of its own sublime Spirit, or free itself entirely from the limitations of sense, form and conditional environments.

Such is life within the boundaries of time, and such is life within the grander realms of eternity, where time hath no existence, but which is always below the grand ideal of the

Divine Ego in man. As the Soul grows and expands within the sunlight of Divinity, its senses become more acute and its attributes more awakened; its knowledge of "*the things that are*" and its powers over "self" becomes more conscious and positive, its limitations and barriers are less, its opportunities and possibilities for the acquisition of the realities of life greater. But there is and will always be comparative limitations, comparative sense conditions and consequently comparative environments, because the human Soul is finite, and cannot transcend itself. Further, Deity is ever in motion and eternally progressive in His infinite scheme of unfoldment and creation, and, though we may, indeed, become in conscious rapport with creative vibration and in some measure attain the Divine at-one-ment with the Father, yet, this at-one-ment is but the responsive harmony between the Soul and its divine center of being, and not the conscious at-one-ment with the Infinite majesty and power of the Deity itself. As John Young saith, "God the Infinite spirit is uncreated, boundless, formless, eternal, alone," and as such is unapproachable and inconceivable by anything less than Himself. Hence is the Divine reality of man's glorious birth-right, Immortality, an unending existence of eternal and conscious progression. The Soul life of man forms a perfect correspondence to the physical existence, it too hath its longings, aspirations, weariness and disappointments, even as the body has; they move within different dimensions of space only, both are real upon their respective planes of manifestation, but the interior plane is more ethereal and spiritual, consequently infinitely more subtle than the exterior planes of sense and matter. There is a constant reaction between the two, and also between the primary vibrations of physical existence implanted at the moment of conception and set in motion at the moment of birth, and ever-varying vibrations which constitute, by reaction, the pains and pleasures of every-day life. Action and reaction are the dual expressions of that great one-life principle which men call Divine Providence because that which is providential is of necessity lawful and being lawful means being in perfect harmony with the anthem of creative life, consequently, we are all creatures of one Divine law and our perfect freedom can only be realized when we are acting in obedience to the laws of universal being.

Freedom exists only as a universal state and, therefore, to free ourselves, or, in other words, to be free from the reactions of matter, we must realize the absolute truth of the Hermetic mantram, which says, "My Soul is one with the universe and my Spirit an emanation from God." The true secret of freedom then, is to attune our Soul sphere until it beats in rhythmic harmony with the universal harmony, in other words, to intensify the vibrations of the physical organism until they accord in perfect symphony with the vibrations of the indwelling Soul. When this desirable state is attained, the Soul awakes unto the external consciousness of life and its environments, and by virtue of such consciousness arouses into action the higher and more interior laws of its being, which in lower states of development are either entirely dormant, or, at best, only partially active; these higher laws do not conflict with those of lower planes of action, they transcend them only by a simple change of vibration, which means endowing them with a different polarity.

At this point, we impinge upon the boundaries of the great occult forces of nature, occult, because hidden from physical sense and also hermetic because secret and eternally sealed from those minds still dominated by the gross laws, appetites and passions of the brute-nature within the physical body. Soul consciousness is the first spiritual realization of the occult forces of nature and this state of the Soul means *will ability*. *Will*, like all other attributes, is an universal force, hence, our capacity to utilize the universal will exists in proportion to our spiritual development in the higher gamut of existence, or in proportion to our degree of sensitiveness in the lower arc of action.

The former means conscious control of the

force, the latter simply means being the irresponsible medium for its transmission; these constitute the two poles of its action and between them lies every phase of mental, magnetic and metaphysical phenomena. To thoroughly realize this, is to grasp the full significance of the occult law, "As it is below so it is above." Occult laws, then, so far as this special course of study is concerned, relate to the higher and more interior qualities of the human constitution, and their reactions are the physical expressions we find in constant manifestations, both in ourselves and in our surroundings. We must, therefore, gain a thorough knowledge of ourselves and be able to conquer all discord and inharmony within, before we attempt to heal our brother who is sick, in other words, we must first of all have removed the beam out of our own eye before we attempt to remove the mote from the eyes of our neighbor. To *know ourselves*, then, is the first rung in the occult ladder of knowledge and, in order to do this, we must know the hidden forces which control and bind us within the planes of physical life.

Man is a world in miniature and contains within himself a perfect scale of notes, and, no matter what key his nature may accord with or vibrate to, he is a perfect gamut if properly sounded; he is a part of the great solar system of which our sun is the center, and, of course, both *it* and *us* are but fractional parts of the still greater Astral system to which our sun belongs and so "ad infinitum." As there are no special laws relating to any individual, no private legislature possible in the Divine economy of creative law, we must be a part of all that transpires in the action and inter-action of the planetary and stellar worlds. Cosmic law must affect us in proportion to our state, as it does the dazzling worlds of space. This being so we must first of all look to those primary centers of force and grasp their power before we attempt to bind and measure the reactions of those powers as they become manifest in ourselves.

With the foregoing before us, we can see that those powers which mould and guide the life of the physical man are the vibrations received from the forces which mould and guide the destinies of worlds, the only real difference being the length of the orbit of action; in our own case, a few fleeting seasons only, in the case of worlds, embracing untold millions of ages. Further, the higher and more spiritual laws which confine their action to the Soul of man and the universe are also the same, for the spiritual life of man forms a perfect correspondence to the spiritual life of the planet, of which he is an atomic part towards an organic whole.

All known physical force has its origin in the sun and is dependant upon solar action for continued activity. The external sun is but an expression of an internal Spiritual center of intelligence, equal in its spiritual force upon the interior planes of life, to the physical orb upon the spaces of matter, and, as the physical sun is demonstrated by science to be the source of all physical life, the Spiritual orb must be the celestial center of our Soul-life and be the source of all divine possibilities.

Solar force and planetary influence are one and the same. The seven planets of the ancients were but the expressions, so to speak, of the perfect scale of force, each planet, being magnetic by means of solar induction, reflected and still reflects one of the great attributes—Saturn, the cold, Jupiter the genial, Mars the fiery, the Sun itself, the majestic and commanding power, Venus the loving influx in nature, Mercury the inventive and commercial principle, and the Moon the negative, mediumistic and maternal attributes. These powers represent states, and incarnate themselves within each organism, they constitute the primary factors of our being, and must be known, if we would obey the Divine injunction, "Man, know thyself." The "modus operandi" of these powers is that of all nature, "Vibration," in fact, the grand basis of all force is vibration, apart from it, there is neither mental activity, divine providence nor physical motion. Vibration is the real source of all phenomena, spiritual, mental and physical. This is no vague dream, it is an absolute fact in nature and one that is daily receiving scientific recognition in different departments of human knowledge. When we grasp this fact and understand that the metaphysical relationship between external form and mental force is that of vibration alone, it will at once enable us to realize that higher truth, viz., that all we can possibly conceive in the dual expression of good and evil are due to the simple action of harmonious or discordant vibrations, either within or without the human organism.

Man is the perfect expression of the forces of nature at the moment of conception and birth, and their harmonies and inharmonies at these times will find expression within his physical organism, and, be the means, in a great measure, of aiding or retarding his spiritual evolution in this stage of human evolution and development. In fact, each human being is, in a representative sense, an instantaneous photograph of the cosmic vibration operating at the moment of birth, his life and actions, in the form of his material destiny, are nature's simple methods of developing the picture. Everything, in fact, depends upon these occult vibrations received from the starry worlds above.

Remember these important facts. The magnetic constitution depends entirely for its strength upon the position of the luminaries at birth, the less inharmony prevaling between the two, the stronger the life force will be, and

CELESTIAL DYNAMICS.

the less liable to suffer from any reactionary forces, termed tendency towards disease. The sun is always electric in its action, and the moon magnetic, all the magnetic states are attractive while the electric states are repulsive. It naturally follows that purely magnetic natures will attract disease, especially so if in a depleted state, while electric natures will repel. This must be borne in mind, because no one should attempt to heal others unless they possess either a surplus vitality or an electric nature. If they disobey this rule they will fail to cure, and, in addition, will attract some portion of the disease, and consequently suffer from inharmony. To all who attempt the healing art divine, the thorough understanding not only of themselves but of the real magnetic natures of their patients becomes thus an absolute necessity. Such understanding is the true secret of success, and in the following pages it is the purpose to reveal these astro-magnetic mysteries, so that the reader may apply the great astrological laws to their own lives and also to arrive for themselves and their fellow men at a fuller realization of Divine truth.

Note: "Upon the Solar ray depends all that is, that was, or ever can be;" realize this from the light within.

CHAPTER II.

THE LANGUAGE OF THE STARRY HEAVENS.

Nothing in nature is dumb, nothing devoid of mind, that which to man seems dumb, inert and lifeless is only apparently so to his dull sense of perception. It is maya, an illusion of matter. Science once again, in its reawakening cycle, is demonstrating each day by means of the microscope, the spectroscope and the camera that all nature is ceaselessly active, not only living and moving but actually glowing with all the intensity of evolutionary life. To live means to possess mind in some differentiated degree, in other words, to possess being and consequently consciousness in some form or other. Life and conscious mentality involve the possession of some form of language peculiar to that particular plane. That form of language is intelligible to man, if he could only place himself enrapport therewith and so understand it, since to man hath been given the dominion over everything both in the heavens above and in the earth beneath, so that the agnostic who answered in the affirmative, the question, "Can matter think," approximated the truth.

To the student of nature, it is a fact that each separate department of nature possesses a language, and also the equally valuable function or attribute of writing and so recording its own history, not as man does, in a biased prejudiced manner, but scientifically exact and eloquent with all the stern grandeur and nakedness of simple truth. The great geological chapters of our earth's past history are profoundly instructive, not so much from the Divine revelation of her genesis and growth there revealed, but for the positive knowledge we obtain of *her future* and ultimate destiny. And as it is with the earth, so is it with the stars, sun, moon and planets. Mathematics and mental power can reveal their past mutations, conjunctions and transmutations at any given period in the past, so also can the same means foretell, to the day and the hour, their relative positions in the universe at any period in the near or remote future. This, in some sense, is the external language of the starry heavens. It is nature's mathematical form of speech. She speaks thus to the human intellect and, so speaking, enables man to assume the mantle of the prophet and predict future events.

But there is a deeper and more mystical language than that comprised within the mathematical alphabet. This interior language speaks to the Soul and the intuitional mind and reveals the invisible harmonies of our astral system produced by the ever varying motions of the gathering worlds in space, and, from these harmonies, the human mind, aided by the responsive intuitions of the Soul, can see and read the reactions, the discords of nature eternally produced in obedience to the universal law of equilibrium.

What, then, is this hidden language, and by what means can we, on earth, not only read heaven's golden alphabet but read the lessons, warnings and revelations aright? It is now our humble duty to answer these questions, and, in doing so, we desire each reader to repeat, and meditate *daily* upon the great Hermetic law, viz.: "That which is on the earth is as that which is above in the sky, and that which is above in the heavens is as that which it below on the earth," or more briefly stated "as it is above, so it is below," by correspondence, this law is an absolute truth throughout every department of nature. This explains the law of correspondences, and is the one grand key to all metaphysical problems.

Occult law and spiritual affinities cannot be mathematically demonstrated in the physical laboratory; the laws and principles which constitute the eternal analogies of nature cannot be reached and understood by any purely external method of experiment and reasoning. This class of phenomena is purely spiritual, occult and mental, and consequently must, for understanding, be explored upon that plane of life. For illustration, take the first and tenth mansions of a celestial chart of birth. (See "The Language of the Stars.") The first house governs the personal affairs, disposition, etc.,

CELESTIAL DYNAMICS.

etc., of the native, while the tenth rules his credit, business, etc. Physical science at once projects the questions, why is that influence, what causes the first house to govern life and the tenth honor, and expects an answer that would explain the *reasons*. We cannot give such an answer, we only know that these are facts, we can prove these statements to be so in the Horoscope of any person living or dead, but we cannot, unfortunately, render the answer in the terms and the manner required by science. Our answer would be symbolical and occult, because the influence is spiritual and mystical, but science would instantly reject such as an evasion, a myth or a dream. In short the "parting of the ways" has been reached, it is necessary to enter the more interior dimensions of human knowledge, where so-called exact science with its limitations and conventionalities cannot at present follow.

Man is a microcosm, a universe in miniature, a perfect epitome of the heavens. The twelve divisions of the solar year, termed signs of the Zodiac, correspond to and find a complete expression in the twelve divisions of the human organism, (see also "The Language of the Stars.") While the twelve Zodiacal constellations possess the same mystical affinity with the incarnated Soul. But there is a wide difference between the two,—*the signs and the constellations*.

Man then must be considered as a complicated digest of universal nature and strung together by force, ever acting and reacting, and also as the recipient of one continual stream of life essence, containing all the contingent properties of physical vitality and spiritual vigor, expansion and growth. This is occultly termed "The *one* life principle." It is, at once, alike, physical strength, spiritual inspiration and the divine "Breath of God," according to the state and plane of its reception. *Remember this fact.*

Further, if man is continually receiving, he must also in return be continually transmitting, and upon his mental state and his Soul aspiration depend the quality of the force which he thus transmits. The purity of desire and the strength of the will are the chief factors. Man may thus give to his fellowman mental poison and physical inharmony, he may give a perfectly negative and useless grade of substance possessing no definite form, (if the will is weak and the mind frivolous), or he may give spiritual life and thus awaken those around him to a realization of Divine strength.

And lastly, if man is continually acting and reacting within himself he must be the point of concentration, because all force *is but vibration*, and such indeed we find him to be; man is but a grand musical instrument, the body the sounding board and the senses the strings which respond to the continuous vibrations set in motion by the sun, moon and planets. The

CELESTIAL DYNAMICS.   27

brain is <u>the highly sensitive medium acting in strict obedience to the harmony</u> or the discord which these vibrations produce. To learn the cause of these is to *know ourselves* and the forces which are continually urging and predisposing us to the various actions which constitute in their sum total the phenomena of daily life.

(1) Firstly then, ever remember that the sun is the primary cause of all life, and the (2) moon is the secondary factor, while the planets fill up the lights and shadows—the details of the picture.

During the twelve solar months, *i. e.* from the sun's entry at the first point of Aries, at the Vernal equinox, until its return to the same place the following year, all the various kinds of human beings are produced *possible* in that cycle. The sun, by its own *real place* and position in the Zodiac shows the primary trend of the mental evolution of the *race*, but by its *apparent annual position* in the Zodiac it shows the *primary trend of the individual man*, while the position of the moon and planets polarizes that force and also reveals the nature and direction of such influx. Therefore, to learn the hidden nature of the forces dominating any given person, it is necessary to understand all the elementary principles of astronomy and astrology, in other words, to become perfectly familiar with the external alphabet of the celestial language. This alphabet consists of the signs or characters of the sun, moon and planets and of the symbols of the twelve zodiacal signs which form the starry pathway in the heavens of those bright ministers of nature's will, Providence.

Presupposing in advance, then, that the student has mastered or committed to memory those external symbols, we commence the first simple forms of that language whose rhythmic vibrations caused the great Samian Sage, Pythagoras, to formulate its nature to his chosen disciples as "the music of the spheres."

There are twenty-two characters or letters in the alphabet, exactly the same number as in the Hebrew which was based upon similar principles. These are the Sun, Moon, Neptune, Uranus, Saturn, Jupiter, Mars, Venus and the planet Mercury; these constitute the vowels and the diphthongs; then come the consonants, Aries, Taurus, Gemini, Cancer, Leo, Virgo, Libra, Scorpio, Sagittarius, Capricorn, Aquarius, and Pisces, known as the signs of the Zodiac, and lastly, the Earth, or ⊕, which is a mere cipher, like the twenty-second letter of Hebrew, in fact, from a symbolical point of view, there is a wonderful affinity between the basic constitution of the two.

To commence with the most important orb, the Sun stands forth as the central force of all. He rules the vital springs of life in man and the love in woman, he rules the heart, and if he is afflicted by Saturn or Mars or Uranus at

CELESTIAL DYNAMICS. 29

birth, the life force or physical vitality will suffer in proportion. His vibrations are electrical, hot, commanding, penetrating and aspiring. In the fiery signs he is most powerful, next in the airy, then the earthy and, lastly, in the watery where he is weakest of all.

The Moon is next in importance, she appears in power as the hand-maid and bride of the Sun, and reigns as the minister of the Solar bounty. She rules the vital force in Woman and the *love* in man. She has chief control of the intuition of both sexes and is most potent in the watery signs, next in the earthy, then in the airy and weakest of all in the realm of fire. She thus stands forth as the polar opposite of the sun, *his other half in nature.* Her vibrations are magnetic, cool, yielding and formative. She rules the breast, stomach and the entire fluidic system of the organism.

The planet Mercury comes forth in capacity of interpreter. Messenger of the gods, he partakes of the character of each and all with whom he is associated by aspect at the moment of birth. His nature is therefore convertible and either good, bad or indifferent as the case may be. To him is given the chief rule of the mental qualities. He polarizes the solar influx in the brain and so gives direction and bias to the external mind. He rules the tongue and nervous system. His vibrations are changeable.

The planet Venus comes next, sweet child of the ocean foam, she stands forth in the starry tongue as the representative of mirth, domestic love, art and music. She is the chief ruler of the internal sex and generative functions of humanity, and has especial influence of a peculiar nature over the group of diseases peculiar to females. She rules the ovaries and the venous system. Her vibrations are magnetic, moisture-producing, warm, producing the ideal and sublime and are also benefic in the second degree.

Mars, the god of war, is our next force and appears as the representative of strife, energy, destruction and combativeness. He has chief rule over the passions and animal appetites and rules the external sexual organism, the muscles and sinews. His vibrations are electrical, fiery, disruptive, sharp and cutting, ever tending to inflammation, opposition and change. He is also malefic in the second degree.

The planet Jupiter stands forth as the symbol of authority, as the social, noble, paternal guide and has chief rule over those functions that establish law, order, commerce and theology. He rules the arterial system of the body and his vibrations are electric, health giving, inspiring, tending to magnanimity in all things and benefic in the first degree.

The planet Saturn stands forth as the symbol of old age, the antithesis of life and vigor,

CELESTIAL DYNAMICS.

he is the harbinger of sorrow, disease and inharmony, and has chief rule over the reflective and reasoning faculties. He rules the bones, liver and spleen. His vibrations are cold and death like, magnetic in nature and malefic in the first degree.

The foregoing constitute the first gamut of notes, they are the seven vowels and from this a higher key is sounded, which we term the diphthongs as they are convertible or double, that is, contain two qualities, as a diphthong contains the double sound of two vowels.

Uranus, the mystery planet, stands as the first orb in the higher octave of force. He is chief ruler of the occult, mystical and metaphysical qualities of man and governs the odyllic sphere, or magnetic aura of the organism, and is therefore representative of all mental, magnetic and occult medicine for the cure of disease. His vibrations are cool, electro-magnetic, and tend to change and reconstruction.

Neptune, the second diphthong stands last in order and also remotest from the sun. His chief rule is over the imaginations and the fair realms of Utopia. His action is upon the mind and never expressed directly upon the physical plane, he expresses the higher or Platonic love in man and his vibrations are also electro-magnetic, like those of Uranus, but more ethereal and also convertible.

For a complete description of the consonants or twelve signs, see part II, of the "Light of Egypt." The last symbol ⊕, is nill in both influence and effect. As before stated, it represents the earth, the passive center of man.

QUESTIONS FOR STUDENTS TO ANSWER.

1. What and whence *is occult force?*
2. How and by what means do we receive Solar power?
3. What constitutes planetary influence?
4. Upon what law or principle does force act and react?
5. What constitutes good, and vice versa,—what evil?
6. How and by what means is this force controling man?
7. By what means can we alter inharmonious forces?
8. How can we obtain freedom from suffering?
9. What constitutes free will?
10. Do we possess free will? if so, how and when?
11. What relations exist between the Zodiac and the physical organism?
12. What is the most difficult thing in this lesson for you to comprehend?

In order to comprehend these lessons fully the student should study the second part of "Light of Egypt," especially chapters I, II, III and IV.

CELESTIAL DYNAMICS. 33

CHAPTER III.

THE VITAL FORCE.

The Vital force, which is the life force which gives strength and action to the physical organism, is a very different essence to that which gives manifestation to the mental and intellectual qualities. The two are totally different and distinct from each other, as may be seen in the case of an idiot enjoying robust physical health and of an intellectual genius with poor health and delicate constitution. But these forces may be capable of expressing a wonderful energy when acting in consort with each other through harmonious co-operation.

The force which we shall deal with principally in this chapter is that quality of the biune life force which relates to physical being, health, strength, and energy of the human body, and which increases, limits, or decreases its powers of function in strict ratio to its strength and tone of vibration.

Before entering upon this very important subject, a few preliminary considerations are necessary. A given organism, which in its sum total constitutes the external clothing or temple of an incarnated Soul, is, according to its degree of evolution, the status or condition in which that Soul is required by nature to exercise its functions.

In order to give being, in the first place, to such an organism, a germ soul or seed containing all the latent potentialities of the future form is necessary. This is supplied by the mother; the electrical or vitalizing current is given by the father. Upon the exact balance of these two depends the perfect balance of the physical human organism of the future child, *we mean* the physical balance, not mental. The intense vibrations set in motion during the conjugal union may cause either intellectual, physical, moral, sensual or the criminal tendencies of nature to become dominant at birth, or, as is most generally the case, a combination of two or more of these qualities. But, springing from the ovum in the womb, the physical organism as it rapidly builds itself together under the evolutionary impulse of the electro-magnetic life force set in motion by the parents, is of itself nothing but a semi-solid wrapper, an aggregation of crystalized atoms which acts as the covering for the electro-vital form which is the true source of *its* strength or weakness.

This form receives and radiates throughout the entire nervous system a special quality or degree of the universal life essence of nature, and it can only absorb and radiate that peculiar grade of such essence which is in perfect rapport with its own special state, plane and polarity, and this grade or status is the *tone*, the *key-note* to which the electro-vital consti-

CELESTIAL DYNAMICS.

tution vibrates and which in turn sets in motion and controls the *responsive vibrations* of the external physical form. This subject alone would fill a volume if dealt with in proportion to its importance and merit; for the present purpose it will suffice to indicate a few self-evident differences in human polarity, due to this difference of electro-vital vibration. Some natures delight in close city life and are only healthy when so situated, others require a rural home, some thrive in a high altitude, a table land, some require the lower plains, others require the swamps and dense forest, some natures can only enjoy good health in the mountains, others require the sea-coast.

Of course, in the artificial life of to-day, the product of applied mental force and under civilized methods of rendering naturally uncongenial localities suitable for habitation, we do not observe this process of "natural selection" carried to any marked extent. It is a fact in nature, nevertheless, and is instinctively followed by simple so-called savage-tribes of people in their choice of a home; on the same principles that affect the migration of birds and beasts. In a natural state, these "children of nature" unerringly seek their congenial habitat, and that selection depends upon the tone of their physical requirements, due to vibration, which is the celestial dynamic energy, expressing itself through their organic natures from birth.

Claudius Ptolemy who flourished during the latter part of the first and the beginning of the second century of the Christian era, and who is justly entitled the father of modern astrology, in aphorism 86, of his great work the "Centiloquium," says, "The Sun is the source of the vital power, the Moon of the natural power," and the astrological experience of all noted professors during the subsequent 1800 years has verified the truth of his brief statement.

The true source of the vital power in man is derived from the Sun. He forms the vitalizing section of humanity, while the true source of the vital power in woman is the moon. She constitutes the *natur-al*, or maternal section of humanity, as *natio*, was the Goddess of birth, and the word 'natural' is derived from "nasco," which means *to be born*. Of course, there are many slight variations from the strict application of this rule, also many combinations of the Sun and Moon interacting with each other, producing in some people not only a strangely dual constitution, but also a luni-solar vitality. These variations will be duly noticed as we proceed.

The primary considerations are, firstly, the cosmic energy exerted by the Sun. In the northern hemisphere, the greatest vitalizing power is from the twenty-first of March until the twenty-first of June. The second grade of force or intensity, is from the twenty-first of

CELESTIAL DYNAMICS.   37

June until the twenty-first of September. The third grade is from December twenty-first until March twenty-first, and the least potential of all the quarters is from September twenty-first until the same date in December when the Sun reaches the lowest point in the cosmic arc of life in the northern hemisphere. Thus, for instance, a child born with a given sign rising in November, will never, all other conditions being equal in the two cases, equal in vitality and strength, another child born under the same sign in April. These are important facts to remember.

Secondly, the signs of the Zodiac have a special force, as mediators, etc., by forming specially favorable conditions, or otherwise, for this life essence to manifest itself in the organism. The fiery and airy or masculine signs, as they are termed, form the strongest conditions in a male Horoscope when rising at birth, while the earthy and watery, or feminine signs, give the best possible conditions in a female natus.

With the foregoing considerations before us, let us now descend to the practical details which are based upon the following rules.

I. The Sun is always hyleg in a male Horoscope by day, *ie*, when the Sun is above the horizon.

II. When the Sun is below the horizon in a male natus the vital force undergoes a change and if the Moon be above the horizon, it becomes a joint ruler of the vital force, rendering a luni-solar vitality.

III. When neither the Sun nor Moon be above the horizon at birth, then the ascendant of the Horoscope becomes the joint ruler of the Native's vital force.

IV. In a feminine Horoscope, substitute the Moon for the Sun and the same rules will apply.

Thus we find that man's vital nature is governed by the Sun alone, when the Sun is able to manifest its own force by being above the horizon. But when not so placed, the Moon, if above the horizon shares this function *with the Sun* giving a luni-solar force, and when neither of the luminaries are above the horizon, the ascendant and the Sun become the givers of life. With a woman the case is reversed. When the Moon is above the horizon, it is the sole ruler of vitality. If not, and the Sun be there, she is under a luni-solar force, and when neither are so situated, she is ruled by the ascendant and the Moon. So that after all, the real vital center of woman is the Moon, and the vital center of man is the Sun, the ascendant being only a point of reaction.

In judging of the strength or weakness of the vital forces operating at birth, proceed as follows:

I. If the hyleg be afflicted by the evil aspects of Uranus, Saturn, or Mars, the life essence will be vitiated in proportion to such affliction.

II. If the hyleg be free from affliction of such malefics the life essence is fairly strong and the life will be of good average duration.

III. If, in addition to the foregoing, the hyleg receives the assistance of benefic aspects from Mars, Jupiter or Venus a good length of life is assured, because the vital forces are intense in their vibrations, and with care a ripe old age may easily be obtained by such a Native.

IV. If, on the contrary, the Hyleg be weak and at the same time much afflicted by the malefic orbs, the vital force is much below nature's requirements and death in infancy is the general result, and, should the ascendant be weak also, an early death is certain. In spite of all Christian, metaphysical and medical science, *death will claim its proper due.*

Claudius Ptolemy, previously quoted, gives an almost infallible rule for fore-seeing death in infancy, viz., "If one of the luminaries be angular and either joined to a malefic, or if the latter be at an equal longitudinal distance from each luminary (that is equi-distant) so as to form an equilateral triangle with them, and no benefic aspecting them at the time, and the rulers of the luminaries be in malefic places, the child then born will not be reared but will shortly die."

To the uninitiated this may seem to be words without meaning, but it is a truth which the author has verified in scores of cases.

All those who attain a ripe old age have the vital points of their Horoscope strong, these are the Sun, Moon and ascendant, and those who die young have them weak.

The physical constitution depends for its strength upon its polarity, and this is determined, firstly, by the sign rising and, secondly, upon the polarity of the Moon. There are many thousands of people with a very strong vitality combined with a somewhat delicate physical constitution, who are always in rather delicate health and "ailing," yet who manage to live to a good old age, while the stout robust looking people around them die off in the very prime of life. Some professors would say that this was due to the "directions" and, while admitting due potency to such arcs of force, yet I have seen apparently powerful physical natures die under the weakest of directions and, *per contra*, I have seen weakly looking mortals survive in spite of the most ominous train of "arcs of directions." Long years of experience and patient research into the hidden *causes* of such discrepancies have revealed to me the fact that the physical constitution and the vital essence thereof *vibrate to different degrees of force*; that, while the Sun and Moon are the dispensers of vital energy, the sign rising at birth and planets therein, if there be any combined with the polarity of the Moon at the time, determines the exact polarity of the physical organism, and, upon

CELESTIAL DYNAMICS. 41

the temperament thus manifested, depends the general physical health. But the vital current of life is not so dominated. This depends solely upon the vital status of the luminaries, chiefly the Sun in man and the Moon in woman, with either the one or the other or ascendant as a simple center of reaction only, when the proper Hylegical luminary is below the horizon.

In all research of an occult or an astrological nature ever remember this law, viz., that the Sun is the one great central fountain of all action and the Moon the parent of *its manifestation*. In other words, the Sun is the father and the Moon the mother of everything and all phenomena that eventuate upon the earth.

42 CELESTIAL DYNAMICS.

CHAPTER IV.

THE TEMPERAMENT, PHYSICAL AND MAGNETIC.

There are two distinct temperaments in man, one purely physical and the other magnetic, and these are due to polarity. The physical temperament is determined by the sign rising at birth along with the planet or planets within that sign, if there be any, and the polarity of the Moon. The masculine signs are electric and the feminine signs are magnetic. Jupiter, Mars and the Sun are also electric in nature, while Saturn, Venus and the Moon are magnetic. Uranus is electro-magnetic and Mercury is either the one or the other according to his condition and aspect at the moment of birth. The temperament will consequently vary according to the influences at work. At this point, a slight digression will tend to a clear understanding.

All strength, whether it be vital, mental, magnetic or physical, depends solely upon the one condition—Harmony. All weakness, on the contrary, depends upon the antithesis of harmony, which we term discord, and according to the status of these two conditions will be the so-called good and evil. In fact, every thing that eventuates within the prescribed limits of our environment, wherein we are compelled by nature to live and move, oscillates between these two simple states of vibration. Life and death, health and disease, happiness and misery, success and failure, mental vigor and imbecility, are the mundane results which spring forth from the action and reaction of the dynamic pendulum of nature in the one eternal ceaseless struggle towards a cosmic equilibrium. This is a most important consideration as affecting "temperament," as will be seen as we proceed.

I. If an electrical sign ascend at birth and the Moon at the same time occupies one of the same nature, the organism will have an harmonious vibration. And of these signs, the fiery give the greatest physical strength, and, further, these conditions are manifested in their greatest intensity in a male horoscope.

II. If the Moon occupies a magnetic sign and a similar sign be rising, the same harmonious results will occur, but of a different character, viz., magnetic, and will manifest their greatest force in the horoscope of a female.

III. Magnetic planets in an electric sign, or electric planets in a magnetic sign, give a dual nature and cause the temperament to be electro-magnetic.

IV. If the sign rising be electric and the sign occupied by the Moon be magnetic, or vice versa, the same dual result in temperament will occur.

V. Sometimes it will be found that the

natures will conflict somewhat. For instance, suppose a person is born with Cancer rising with the planet Mars in that sign, and, at the same time, the Moon occupies a magnetic sign, we have an electro-magnetic ascendant and a magnetic polarity for the Moon. Now, if such an instance transpired in the natus of a female, the temperament would be magnetic, because the external force is more magnetic than electric, and females incline to, or, are naturally of the magnetic polarity, and the balance of power would, therefore, be given to the feminine force. But, on the contrary, if such a case was a male natus, the temperament would be electro-magnetic because man inclines towards the electric element in nature and would lend his own natural powers to this plane and form the balance.

Having given the general rules we will now briefly examine the particulars in forming a correct judgment.

Firstly, then, pay particular attention to the sign rising; this sign, if there be any planet therein, will give the correct physical temperament. Fiery signs give a dry caloric temperament. Earthy signs give a cool phlegmatic temperament. Airy signs give a volatile nervous temperament, while the watery signs produce a cold lymphatic temperament. Then secondly, add to this the nature of the planet or planets in the rising sign, and that one which is located nearest to the cusp of the ascendant will predominate over all the others in its external action upon the organism.

If there should be no planet in the ascending sign, observe the Moon, and combine the influence of the Moon (without any regard to her aspects) with the sign rising, and the correct physical temperament will be obtained. The reason we ignore the lunar aspects in this case is because the aspects affect the mind, and not *the external* temperament which we are now considering. And these two are very different or distinct factors, in the system we are now elucidating, viz., the metaphysics of astrology and not the exoteric, orthodox science of the ordinary astrological professor who usually knows absolutely nothing of the higher aspects—the celestial dynamics of his peculiar prognostic art.

From what has been stated regarding the electric and magnetic natures of the signs and planets, it will be very easy for the student to discover whether a person be of electric, magnetic or electro-magnetic temperament. This is of great importance or value in *healing and treating*. A few more considerations upon this point are needed. Electric natures repel ideas and thoughts unless they *appeal to their inner natures*, and they never become dominated by them. On the contrary, magnetic natures attract thoughts and ideas and very soon become dominated by them, and if not, they always assimilate them in some form or other, while electro-magnetic natures alternately attract and repel, they do not possess true consistency, they are all one thing under one state or condition, and are quickly all enthusiasm for something else directly the attracting current is withdrawn. They delight in the mental whirl of the day and obtain their degree of satisfaction therefrom, until something new or more attractive turns their changeable volatile natures in another direction.

It only remains now to point out how to gauge the real disposition of a person, not their external or apparent natures, but the reality of the real inner self which cannot be bounded by written law, customs, or the conventional usages of society. Perhaps an illustration of our meaning will aid the reader. For instance, a man that will deliberately steal another person's ideas for the purpose of passing them off before the world as his own, and gaining benefit thereby, is just as much a deliberate thief as the criminal who robs a bank or picks a pocket. Equally so is the man or woman who will maliciously rob a person of their reputation and character, or create strife between relations and companions for some dishonest motive, and thus steal a person's friendship from them. This kind of theft is the worst of all, as Shakespeare recognized when he wrote "But he who filches from me my good name robs me of that which not enriches him and makes me poor indeed," so with morality, thousands of advanced minds cannot endure the thoroughly artificial code of morality recognized by society, they defy it and follow a code of their own more in accordance with their peculiar plane of life. The world considers such people heretics of dangerous immorality, whereas they are generally the most thoroughly moral people of their time, in an ethical sense. Morality is a question of principle, not of obedience to a sham or an appearance. Hundreds of thousands who are rigid supporters of the regulation proprieties of society are notoriously immoral in their private relationships. Therefore in guaging the disposition it must be understood that the revelations of this science must be considered in an ethical sense, because they have an ethical value only, and may not exactly tally with the opinion and appearance of the person under consideration.

Carefully apply the following rules:

I. Note down the physical and vital temperament.

II. If they agree in nature, it shows a strong moral bias, but if they conflict in nature, it shows the contrary.

III. Note the condition of the Sun and Moon, if they are afflicted by Uranus, Saturn or Mars without any benefic assistance to counteract such affliction, then the moral bias is weak.

IV. If the influences are good and evil combined, then the person will follow out the conditions in which they find themselves, moral, immoral, or both in turn, as the conditions require.

V. If the temperaments agree and the Moon is free from affliction, and the Sun also free, it shows a very powerful moral bias, a rigid sense of duty.

VI. When the temperaments are harmonious, and the Sun and Moon free from evil aspects, and at the same time in friendly aspects with each other, it shows the very highest conditions. Such a person becomes extremely sensitive of his obligations and would become a patriot to his country and suffer martyrdom for what he considered right.

The general nature and line of active expression that the foregoing would assume will depend upon many conditions; the mental qualities, the plane of life in which the person is born, and education, will each have a great influence, but the chief of these will be noticed in future chapters, and especially in our next, when the manifestation of the disposition in its relation to the mental status will be considered.

CHAPTER V.

THE MENTAL AND INTELLECTUAL POWERS.

Among every generation of astrologers it has been an undisputed axiom that the mental qualities of the child born depend chiefly upon the position of Mercury and the Moon. But, like all general truths, this axiom is only relatively true. Undoubtedly, the combined influence of these two bodies exert a powerful influence upon every human being. This point is not disputed, but the external manifestation of such influence is subject to wonderful variations and modifications. In different individuals, the very same aspects, with the same relative positions to each other, will produce widely different mental results. To assert, for instance, that the conjunction or sextile of Venus to Mercury confers artistic talent or musical ability, while generally true in a majority of cases, may be wholly erroneous in some particular nativity. So, also, Mercury, rising at birth, does not always confer literary power or scientific skill. Such a position is only one of the chief factors of mental superiority, but in order to become active, it must be in unison with the whole mental organism.

To account for the great disparity of mental and moral bias emanating from apparently similar positions of the heavens, many otherwise talented astrologers are now drifting into the fatal error of the theory of *re-birth*. If this theory is correct, scientific astrology is impossible, and its usefulness vanishes into the thin air of incomprehensible metaphysics. Fortunately, however, it is not necessary for the student to fall back upon the unverifiable delusion of reincarnation in order to account for genius. "Past earth lives" and the cumulative effect of a previous karma upon the mental, moral and financial status of the present embodied individuals are, of all the speculative follies in which the undeveloped human mind has indulged, the most insidious and ensnaring, especially to the half awakened Souls who possess a natural love for occult and metaphysical studies; they see as through a glass darkly, and feel satisfied that the half understood subtleties of oriental dogmas rationally solve the problem of good and evil, mental genius and mediocre brains. All such mystical illusions, however, are incapable of passing the only real test we can accept, viz., *genuine proof*. At most, such theories can amount to nothing more than matters of personal opinion, and, as a scientific investigator, the author challenges the ingenuity of man to distil one atom of common sense into the vagaries and metaphysical subtleties of reincarnation or the speculative phantasmagora of its accompanying absurdities. To the earnest searcher after facts, who is free from the subtle intoxication of Oriental Hermeneutics, such theories are interesting only as distorted pictures which, during the processes of evolution, represent the strange aberrations of the human mind.

Those who have eyes to see, and brains to understand the things which they do see in astrological science will readily come to the conclusion that the heavens furnish the key to all apparent contradictions in the mental, moral and financial expressions of the sons of men. Nothing eventuates as the offspring of chance, universal law reigns, but this law is only applicable to *universals*, not to particulars. Particulars, in the affairs of life, are not the offspring of the stars only; indirectly, they spring into being as the outcome of action and reaction between individuals and may be called the fruits of human association. Herein comes into play *man's free will*. Capacity is the measure of free will and *ability* the exact limit of his obligation. Outside these conditional limits the human Soul incurs no responsibility. Remember these facts, they are the secrets of good and evil.

The mental and intellectual qualities depend upon the polarity of the brain and temperament of the physical organism. This latter has been fully explained in the last lesson, the present remarks will be confined to the former.

The position of the Sun and Moon determines the brain polarity in all cases. The planet Mercury shows by his position and aspect *the native* qualities of the intellectual force. When the Moon is in aspect to Mercury, she always points out the individual peculiarities of this force. Benefic aspects give the mental forces an harmonious, moral, generous, bias. Malefic aspects the opposite. George Peabody, the philanthropist, and Thomas Carlyle are fine types of the extremes of the benefic force and discordant rays. Peabody looked upon each human being as his brother. Carlyle could only see the perturbations of human life. In the latter's estimation, Great Britain contained "thirty millions of people, *mostly fools.*" To view the failings of our neighbors with a microscope, and those of ourselves or friends through the large end of a telescope, is a sign of a distorted mentality, the result of the malefic aspects of the heavens at the moment of birth externally, but which originated within the inharmonious spheres of our parents at the moment of conception, upon the interior planes of our vital expression.

The general formula for determining the mental and intellectual qualities is, therefore, as follows: The polarity of the Sun and Moon at the time of birth gives the exact polarity of the brain. This polarity combined with the temperament represents the individual capacity of the native. The aspects of Mercury

CELESTIAL DYNAMICS. 53

and the Moon combined with the influence of any planet (if there be such) rising near the ascendant, represent the individual *ability*. The sum of these two conditions embrace the total of human life in its mental and intellectual expression. It will be apparent, therefore, that a person may possess large capacity for knowledge or art, but may not possess the ability to express this capacity in the external form, while, *per contra*, a person may have a very limited capacity combined with very large ability for expression, such a combination will *express* the utmost possible to such a brain, and its possessor will be rated at more than his true worth, and vice versa. But, when we find a large capacity combined with an equally large administrative ability, then we find true genius, the nature of which will correspond exactly to the plane occupied by the native, the finer the conditions the greater the genius: A section of hell is always necessary in the physical residuum of true genius. It is the spice which gives it flavor.

In order to gauge the polarity of the Sun and Moon it is necessary for the student to thoroughly understand the exact nature of each of the twelve signs upon the intellectual plane. (These are described fully in part second of "The Light of Egypt.") No other plane must be taken into consideration. Further, it must be understood that each sign represents a section of the physical constitution, which has a metaphysical correspondence with the mental principles. This is why people born under different signs contact or sense things, actions, motives and surroundings from different standpoints or planes, consequently those born under the same triplicity generally agree upon general outlines, but differ in particulars denoted by the special signs. The twelve different planes from which the different polarities of the brain react, are as follows:

Aries disposes the brain to sense things from the logical, scientific plane destitute of *feeling*

Taurus, from the cautious, rational, material planes of sense and appetite; it is non-commital.

Gemini, from the volatile, ideal, executive and purely intellectual plane of action.

Cancer, from the formative, sensitive, reflective and maternal planes of action.

Leo, from the heart, the love instincts, and the emotional planes of action.

Virgo, from the aspirational, the sympathetic and the compassional planes.

Libra, from the equalizing instincts, also the sublime and sentimental planes of action.

Scorpio, from the passional or animal instincts, also the sexual and conjugal centers.

Sagittarus, from the migratory instincts also the impulsive (thoughtless) and conventional planes.

Capricorn, from the diplomatic and the selfish but cautious, reflective planes.

Aquarius, from the metaphysical conception and the intuitional plane.

Pisces, from the spiritual or Soul center, in its highest expression, in gross natures, from the magnetic, irresponsible or mediumistic plane.

How to Restrain Criminal Tendencies.

A few words of advice and warning upon the subject of this chapter are in order:

Realize the fact that there is no such thing as radical evil. Evil, so called, is only discordant vibration which requires tuning up to the proper pitch, to so express it, in order to act in unison or harmony with the rest of the organism. There can be no criminal tendency that is not a distortion of some beautiful function. Age and the adverse environments may, of course, so crystallize these conditions that human effort is useless. It is not for those who have passed the age of maturity that these instructions are written, but for the salvation of the young, the rising generation who govern the future.

When, from the Horoscope, evil conditions of the mind are perceived, consult a practical phrenologist, note the organ expressing this astral discord, and then set earnestly to work to alter such, by cultivation and education of the opposite forces. Constantly hold the child in the mental image of exactly opposite tendencies. In time, this mental action will completely polarize the criminal or disordered trait. Mental power continually exercised over the growing immature brain will crystallize all the inharmony and render such function practically nil in later life.

The mental image projected by the metaphysician will take root and grow and ultimately like a good graft upon some worthless seedling bear fair and lovely fruit. Ever remember that whatever is, is good, undeveloped though it be.

CHAPTER VI.

The Financial Prospects.

These depend chiefly upon the harmony by which we find the luminaries surrounded at birth, and the harmonious or discordant conditions of the meridian have also much influence upon finance. These are the principal or primary factors, but, to thoroughly understand their true import, we must penetrate below the external husk and discern the why, the how and the wherefore of such celestial influence. A careful study of Chapter five, Part II of the "Light of Egypt," will show the student that man as the microcosm has an alchemical or mineral constitution, in other words, that we each possess a certain mineral status. This mineral quality represents our *money getting force*. If, therefore, we find the chief rulers of the two precious metals which represent hard cash, silver and gold, the Sun and Moon, discordant and weak in our horoscope, we may rest assured that we do not possess the affinity necessary to acquire wealth.

The forces are attractive and diffusive, attractive and accretive, negatively repellent and positively repellent, according to conditions.

When the mineral vibrations within us are positively repellent, we remain in poverty all through life, when negatively repellent we remain comparatively poor, but do not suffer actual poverty. When the vibrations are attractive and have the polarity of accretion we amass wealth, when the forces are attractive and diffusive we obtain much money during life, but, almost in spite of our best efforts, it goes as fast as it comes, we become spend-thrifts and saving is the last thing we can do.

Remember the important fact, then, that each living individual has some peculiar mineral quality within which vibrates in unison with some natural source of wealth and, of course, is equally antagonistic to some other grade. To discover this quality and apply our efforts to this department of nature is to secure the very highest results, financially, that this life can yield. It is equally and exactly upon this basis that certain geographical locations are fortunate for some individuals and unfortunate for others. The mineral quality of the magnetic currents in the earth agreeing or harmonizing with a person render him what is called fortunate, that is, there is financial harmony. Bad luck so called, is financial discord.

As illustrative of the foregoing, the facts of the two following cases significantly dissimilar, are within the writer's personal knowledge. An English gentleman was in very cramped circumstances, was always unfortunate and failed in everything he undertook in his native country. He emigrated to Australia, comparatively penniless, but, apparently, leaving his usual misfortune in the land of his birth, for he became lucky, married well and was soon quite rich. A French gentleman, born near La Vende, came to England, after trying everything in his own country without success, he started out as a waiter in a French restaurant, finally became the proprietor and got rich. He returned to France to live upon his means and through local investments, quickly lost everything he possessed.

The instances of people, penniless and often poverty stricken, who, emigrating from Europe to the United States of America, and there becoming rich and often amassing great wealth are numerous enough. That may be regarded as a natural consequence, yet many remain in circumstances scarcely superior to those of their native land, while the inequalities of fortune attaching to apparently similar conditions are well known. On the other hand, numerous instances are in the writer's knowledge of native born Americans who could hardly live because of their unfortunate surroundings in America, yet who, on emigrating to England, became fortunate and well to do. Such facts require something more than that convenient scapegoat, coincidence, to explain away. The true reason is their mineral status agreed with the magnetic currents of the country they removed to.

The definite rules, or rather methods, of procedure in the consideration of financial prospects is to first ascertain whether the native is attractive or the reverse. Thus, if the luminaries are strong and well aspected, and the second house and the midheaven unafflicted, and Jupiter and Venus unafflicted, the native's mineral constitution is powerfully attractive. If, in such a case, Mars aspect the luminaries, or be in the second or tenth house, the native is diffusive, the stronger Mars is the more diffusive the native becomes. If Saturn is strong and unafflicted and aspect the luminaries, or be in the second or tenth house, the native's mineral quality is full of accretion, he saves and increases what he gets, and so acquires wealth. The second or tenth house, occupied by Venus or Jupiter, and they strong and unafflicted and aspecting the luminaries, give the very highest conditions for financial success. But, on the contrary, when the Sun and Moon are weak, afflicting each other or afflicted by others, then the quality of vibration is antagonistic to riches, if, at the same time, Saturn or Mars, or both of them be much afflicted and in the second or tenth house and afflict the Sun or Moon, the native will remain perpetually poor and had better be contented with his lot.

From the foregoing, it will be seen that the second house of the horoscope, the meridian, or tenth as it is called, with the Sun and Moon, comprise the foundation, the basis of the native's fortune, while the planets by their condition, position and aspects point out the results. Jupiter and Venus give financial success, when strong, through trade and professional patronage, Mercury, through mental and intellectual exertions, Mars, through military or mechanical efforts where fire and steel are used, Saturn, through mining and the offspring of the ground.

The details of all these are given fully in "The Language of the Stars."

It will be noticed that Mars squanders wealth, while Saturn either hoards it up or prevents the native from getting any at all. Under no circumstances can Saturn make a prodigal nor Mars a miser. So Jupiter, though giving wealth through patronage, merchandise, etc., when afflicted, wastes substance by carelessness, or lack of business habits, etc., as much as by bad judgment in using money.

There are, naturally, many degrees between these extremes, cases wherein the influences are balanced and others in which they may be extended a little either one way or the other; to judge these requires long experience and continued observation.

In order to command all the possibilities of success which nature gives, the temperament and mental qualities must, first, be carefully borne in mind, then, the harmony or discord of the financial nature must be considered, and, lastly, the careful combination of all these elements will indicate the natural department of life for which the native is best adapted. If the tenth is afflicted, the native should never go into business on his own account, he will always succeed best in the employ of others. If the second is afflicted, he should never leave one situation until another is ready, otherwise suffering may ensue. If the tenth is strong and benefics therein, that quality of employment should be chosen that harmonizes with the Sun and the tenth. For instance, if Taurus was upon the meridian and Jupiter in the tenth house and at the same time not in aspect with the Sun, but Venus in friendly aspect, choice should be made of some employment which combine the nature of *Venus* in its *quality* and of *Jupiter* in its *methods*; whereas, if Saturn was afflicted in the tenth, the native should avoid all Saturnine occupations unless he desires to taste misfortune.

These instances will suffice to show the procedure; practice is necessary to become expert. For the various details of business qualifications and the choice of employments, reference may be made to "The Language of the Stars," Page 14, et seq.

A few remarks upon the subject of speculation, will fittingly close this chapter. Whenever the fifth house of the horoscope is occupied by a malefic, or the luminaries are afflicted, speculation must always be strictly avoided. If a horoscope is naturally an unfortunate one, the same remarks will apply. If the malefics are afflicted and occupy the tenth or second house without any counteracting testimony, nothing but loss can come from speculation.

On the contrary, a benefic well aspected in the fifth, especially if it is also the lord of the fifth or rules the Sun or Moon and is in aspect therewith, indicates good fortune in speculations and risky enterprises. When no planets occupy the fifth, but when the lords of the second and fifth houses are in good aspect to each other and to the luminaries, gain by speculation may be expected; and, lastly, when the lord of the fifth, is a benefic, and strong in the tenth or second, it is a strong sign of success through speculation.

CHAPTER VII.

Love and Marriage.

Perhaps one of the greatest boons to humanity is that of a happy marriage, and yet how very few happy unions there are in comparison to the number of marriages. The history of divorce is the record of human ignorance and folly. True love between husband and wife means noble and virtuous children, if the parents are not wicked or impure, and possess interior aspirations. It would be safe to assert that, if all marriages were based upon love, with wisdom in selection of partners, radical crime would disappear from the earth in a single century. Ignorance alone is the grim monster of human suffering. A knowledge of natural law is absolutely essential to harmony, and, natural law, when traced upon the lines of physical manifestation only, is very apt to deceive us with its myriad delusions. To be certain of our knowledge we must trace this law beyond the limits of the planet upon which it is manifest and learn the secret of its origin in the starry heavens. Then and then only can we truthfully say "Whom God hath joined together, let no man put assunder." *Amen*.

There are vital occult laws of sex underlying the conjugal union that man scarcely dreams of as yet, laws which determine the

CELESTIAL DYNAMICS.

mental, moral and financial bias of the offspring which may be the outcome of that union. Each month, as the physiological lunar cycle is completed, the Soul sphere of the woman receives an influx of the life germs passing onward seeking material incarnation. They each possess peculiar qualities to themselves, no two are exactly alike though many may be similar. During the marital act, the exact mental and moral polarity of the parents strikes an instantaneous impression upon the embryonic Soul, which becomes indrawn within the fiery magnetic vortices of the sextual excitement. This impression gives definite traits and potentialities to the latent impersonal monad. To round out the apparently accidental polarity impressed upon it at the moment of its physical conception within the mother's womb requires a certain series of material environments as well as a certain series of mental, moral and financial experiences. At the same time, there is always a correspondence *in nature* between the polarity with its consequent physical requirements and experience and the latent impersonal Soul qualities and their externalizing possibilities. It is, however, quite unnecessary that the sensuous qualities should externalize themselves in criminal form, and the fact that they do so only shows the ignorance or depravity of the spiritual natures of parents.

Any form of vice is only a distorted image of some laudable quality. That is a fact to be constantly borne in mind. The fact that the so-called animal nature of the present generation is so generally depraved is nature's indisputable evidence that the human Soul in its direct action upon the human organism is out of focus. We must each, individually, attune our inner life—the higher self—until it can vibrate in unison with the external form.

Pure love, pure thoughts, spiritual aspirations and a complete image of a noble ideal in the mental sphere of both parents during the conjugal union will, if conception transpire, bring forth corresponding children and they will become the living pictures of the parents' mental image. This is the secret for the regeneration of the race. It is the one grand foundation for the practical and complete upliftment of humanity. This power is chiefly in woman's hands. Verily, only through the noble Soul of woman can man hope for redemption.

The first principle to be observed is that of triplicity. A person born under a fiery sign will always sympathize with those born under similar signs; such a fiery nature, to be happy, must be united to one of the same trigon or its affinity, by affinity, we mean the next quality to it. For instance, air and fire agree. When a fiery sign rises upon the horizon, an airy sign is always setting; this western horizon is the seventh house, which rules love and marriage. So also water and earth are in affinity with each other. Fire cannot burn without air, neither can water exist without earth. At the same time, the perfect rapport is formed only by the same triplicity. Those born under the element of water will find their most perfect counterpart with a similar sign rising, but fire and water, earth and air are the natural base of antagonism.

From the foregoing, the student can quickly see *whom* to love. The question as to when to consumate this love is denoted by the arcs of directions. Never court or marry when suffering from the rays of evil arcs, or disappointment will surely be the result, unless the horoscope is a strong one. But, when the Moon and Venus in the man's, or the Sun and Venus in the woman's, receive the friendly power of the planets, or the ascendant or mid-heaven, take mother nature's hint, open the flood-gates of your heart and let the Goddess in.

We must now consider the horoscope of birth. Should there be any planet within five degrees of the cusp of the seventh house, such a position will indicate the nature of the partner to marriage *but may not* describe the personality. In some cases it will do this, especially if Venus or the Moon be so situated. The first thing to notice in the male natus is the position and power of Venus and the Moon. If these be unafflicted then the native may hope for happiness in marriage, but if they are afflicted by Uranus, Saturn or Mars, then the native is sure of a great deal of trouble in his love affairs, and, if, in addition to this, one of the foregoing planets occupy the seventh he had better never get married, unless the horoscope of the intended wife has Jupiter strong in the same position. When benefics occupy the seventh unafflicted, it is a sure indication of domestic harmony and, of course, vice versa. with this rare exception. viz. If only one malefic occupy the seventh, and he be strong and well aspected by the benefics, and the Sun or Moon, as the case may be, happiness may then result. But this peculiar combination is not often found. For a female substitute the Sun for the Moon, and otherwise judge exactly on the same lines.

When the Moon or Venus in a male natus, or the Sun and Venus (either one or both) be afflicted by Uranus, such a position indicates that some illicit connections will be formed either before or after marriage in the case of a female, and *both* before *and* after in the case or a male. Mars in the seventh signifies that the husband or the wife will be hasty, jealous and passionate. Saturn in the seventh, that the partner in marriage will be cold, melancholy and sickly, or penurious and fretful. Jupiter in the seventh indicates a most happy married life. Venus therein pre-signifies that the conjugal union will be pleasant, loving and joyous and that the partner will be graceful amiable and courteous. When the Sun and Venus in a female horoscope are configurated with Jupiter, or Venus be in the same declination as the Sun much true love and consequent happiness is indicated, while the Moon and Venus in a male figure well aspected by Jupiter render the same conditions.

As a general rule, the student must notice in a male natus what planet the Moon forms the first complete aspect with after birth, then the planet and the sign it occupies will indicate the condition of the future wife, that is the first *liability* to marry. If it be an evil aspect, it should be avoided. If the Moon apply closely to more than one planet a liability to more than one marriage is indicated, if the rest of the indications argue a plurality of wives, and the number of planets indicate the number of marriages. This, however. is only to be considered when the Moon, having completed one aspect, is at the same time within the orb of operation of the other. For instance, if the Moon be nine degrees from a sextile of Jupiter and seventeen degrees from the trine of Saturn, the native has two prospective wives unless indeed he is wise enough to be warned by his planets and refuse a second union. Such a combination implies that, the Moon applying first to Jupiter, shows a noble, warm-hearted woman and a happy marriage, while the second, indicated by Saturn, would be cold natured, of reserved, repining disposition. Vice versa, if Saturn comes first, wisdom would suggest passing him by and waiting for the genial partner indicated in the natus.

A recent author very truly remarks, "For males, have regard to the Moon and Venus, if these be strong and free from affliction of Saturn, they will marry early in life, especially so if they be oriental. But if Saturn afflict the Moon and Venus in a male natus, marriage is delayed, and if the latter be weak, will not occur at all *if Saturn at the same time be strong.*" To this we will add that if Saturn afflict the Moon by powerful aspect, death of the wife is indicated, and if when the aspect is completed the Moon be in a double bodied sign, *ie.*, Gemini, Sagittarius and Pisces, the native will marry again. The planet Uranus afflicting the Moon indicates illicit connections and final separation, and if the lord of the seventh be afflicted, or a malefic be located in the seventh at the same time, divorce is certain to follow marriage. The same will hold good in regard to a female by substituting the Sun for the Moon, in fact the very worst indication in a lady's horoscope is the affliction of the Sun by Uranus, as they always become unfortunate in their love affairs unless counteracted by very strong benefic forces.

We now offer a few words of advice regarding this most important subject. When a person's natus indicates radical misfortune in the conjugal state the wisest course is not to marry at all as "one ounce of prevention is worth a pound of cure." But where the evil is not radical, that is to say, where it is caused by the mere accidental position of a malefic in the seventh house. then the native may marry and live perfectly happy, if there are other good testimonies; as if the partner should have either Jupiter or Venus therein, because the secondary good of the one counteracts the secondary evil of the other. But no secondary influence can overcome radical evil as denoted by the affliction of the Sun, Moon and Venus, and when such transpires in the two horoscopes, always sincerely advise those individuals not to marry, or they will rue it bitterly. The only way to counteract this radical evil of one horoscope is to become united to one whose nature, spiritual and magnetic, forms a perfect affinity of Soul fusion and whose horoscope in this direction contains nothing but the good. But this rare jewel is *very, very* hard to find.

A few words regarding offspring and we bring this section to a close. Solomon says that "there is a time to every purpose under the heavens," and this is especially so in the conception of offspring. When good directions are operating in the wife's horoscope and other conditions are equal is the time for such a sacred purpose. June, July and August are the finest months for conception, especially when the Sun is passing through Cancer and Leo, viz., June twentieth to August twenty-first, and of all times about the tenth of July is best.

Morning unions are more potent than evening, as the body is reinvigorated by rest. A child so conceived would be born with the Sun in Aries in its exaltation, the most vital condition possible as Aries rules the brain and upon this the solar influx is concentrated at this period, while at the moment of conception it was passing through the *heart, Leo, or the breast,* giving the basis of love and human nature so much needed in the noble form of man.

CHAPTER VIII.

FRIENDS AND ENEMIES.

The constant expression of force which we term personal experience in the form of friendship and enmity, the sympathy and antipathy of people, is derived from the attractions and repulsions of our magnetic constitution. It is either electrical or magnetic according to the natural temperament of the individual. Similar natures are attracted to each other. In the case of man and woman, the magnetic force of Venus powerfully attracts the electricity of Mars and vice versa, so that if Mars in one of the horoscopes occupies the place of Venus in the other, mutual love at first sight almost is the sure result, and, as a rule, such a couple would love each other until death separated them.

Those born under the same triplicity are in natural harmony, unless planets occupy the ascendant to interfere. For instance, suppose one person be born with Venus rising in Cancer, another with Saturn rising in the same place. These persons would not agree. The nature of Venus would be unsuited to the nature of Saturn and this opposition or antipathy would be still more strongly marked in influence if Mars and Saturn were so pitted against each other.

The correct time to accurately ascertain the occult and magnetic relationship of others to us, is upon the occasion of the first meeting. The sensations then and there produced are infinitely more keen, clear and distinct than at any subsequent time. It is the first physical contact and the natural effect produced on the odylic sphere is easily read. Afterwards, we become more or less polarized to each other and the sensations are less defined.

In this connection, however, a serious error is frequently made by most sensitives, an error all must earnestly strive to avoid. Merely because antipathy, or even repugnance, is experienced on first contact with a person, the conclusion that such person is evil-minded or impure is not necessarily warranted. His nature may be a sounding board, from which our own selfishness or impurity is reflected back to ourselves. Only after we have become thoroughly just within ourselves and are conscious of self purification and of the certainty that the Soul sphere within is clear and innocent, can we absolutely trust our own sensitive sensations when coming in psychic rapport with others.

The basis of all forms of friendship, (not merely personal, selfish or commercial interests) is the interaction of our planetary natures upon each other, so that two radically antagonistic natures, no matter how good and just they may be individually, can never truly benefit each other. They will differ in opinion, in taste and in their method of judgment, and, for all purposes in life, they are much better apart than together.

Considered astrologically, the eleventh house pre-signifies friends, the seventh house open or business opponents, the twelfth house the native's sorrow and his private secret foes. If a benefic occupy the eleventh unafflicted, it shows good and faithful friends. If benefics occupy the seventh and twelfth also unafflicted, it indicates that the native will have very few, if any, enemies of any kind. On the contrary, malefics posited therein indicate the exact reverse, and, the more afflicted they may be, the greater the evil arising therefrom.

The foregoing will prove true to some extent in every nativity but must be accepted more as symbolical and apparent than radical and real. That is to say, planets so situated symbolize those things, but everything depends upon the real strength of the horoscope as a whole and upon the benefic power of the luminaries. A really fortunate native will suffer very little from the mere fact that Saturn or Mars are located in the eleventh or twelfth house, unless they, at the same time, afflict the Sun and Moon. On the other hand, an unfortunate native with such a position might suffer severely. Malefics in the seventh, however, always possess very great power, no matter how fortunate the native may otherwise be. For this reason, they are angular and stand, sentinel like, as the evil genius over our matrimonial and domestic relations and business partnerships. Such a position creates misunderstandings between people and brings discord always.

In all cases, the vital question as to the native's friends must be determined more or less by the luminaries. If these orbs be evilly placed and badly aspected, the native will possess but few friends in life and a great many enemies and this will be intensified if there be a malefic in one of the houses before mentioned, because it will then have a radical base to work on. When such is the case and the malefic occupying such house afflict the luminaries he becomes one of the most unfortunate of mortals. On the other hand, if the Sun and Moon be oriental and well aspected and the benefics well elevated above the malefics the native will have but few foes and a host of helpful friends who will always be ready to aid and assist him.

From personal experience, I have noticed that men who have the Sun afflicted by Mars suffer very much from the criticism and slander of others, and that females who have the Moon so afflicted suffer in the same way; that Mars, when afflicting either luminary in a natus, gives much liability to criticism and slander, and further, that Saturn afflicting the lights, especially the Moon in a male or the

Sun in a female natus, indicates suffering by or through friends, either from actual deceit or by being led astray through their association or advice. These are facts for the student to remember and carefully apply.

In order to know the people with whom to associate in life, note the planet or planets which constitute the good in the horoscope, (even Saturn, Mars and Uranus are good if strong and quite unafflicted and at the same time well aspected,) choose such people as these good indications denote and, vice versa, avoid all that are symbolical of the evil of our nativity.

We possess the power to shun the evil and to choose the good, we need not associate with any nature which we know is detrimental to our life, health or interests. We ought to be sufficiently the master of ourselves to avoid being drifted with the current of social conventionalism into the society of those with whom we cannot possibly harmonize or generously agree without being false to our higher selves and indulging in pure cant for the sake of saying something polite. Remember that of all forces in the universe which concern human happiness and mental purity, the magnetism of our associates is the most potent in its effects upon our lives. The mental contagion of an impure mind or the personal poison that we receive from an impure Soul cannot possibly be estimated at its true significance. Some of the greatest crimes in the world have emanated from such contact. Mental poison corrupts good morals, it warps sound judgment and often makes a complete wreck of life.

CHAPTER IX.

CELESTIAL DYNAMICS IN OPERATION.

When we consider the universal harmony of nature, the mutual dependence of all its various parts upon each other, and the continuous inter-action of each atom upon each as units, and upon the whole, it becomes evident that there can be no such thing as accident or chance. There is no room within the divine economy, infinite as it is, for anything but one grand chain of sequences, the outcome of that divine One life termed Providence. All apparent accidents are the reactions of preformulated ideas, all fortuitous chances are the natural lawful outcome of previously active forces set in motion in obedience to the internal laws of life, and their external appearances, strange at times though they seem, are the legitimate results swung into objective existence within the arc of the mighty pendulum of cause and effect.

Nothing eventuates without cause, nothing transpires without effect, so likewise nothing can exist without fulfilling a set purpose within the divine scheme of creation. Hence, whatever is is good, is lawful, is in obedience to the creative fiat and is a part of God's providence.

The first fatal step a metaphysician takes is also the last one, viz., a denial of objective fact. The primary fundamental error of all subsequent errors is made in the denial of the reality of physical expression upon the plane of physical life. There is an inconceivable difference between physical expression and physical causation, for, as an abstract or metaphysical truth, there can be no such thing as physical causation, seeing that physical nature, as we understand objective phenomena to be, is but the reflection of subjective causes, differing in both quality and degree. But expression is one of the grandest facts of evolutionary life and to understand this phenomena, no matter whether it represents a full blown rose or the sorrow and suffering of disease, we must first acknowledge its physical objective reality upon its own plane of manifestation *ie.*, the plane of crystalized appearances and the plain upon which we, as embodied mortals, are compelled to exercise our various functions.

It is a real thing no matter how transitory and unreal it may be when viewed from the interior plane of the Soul.

As a general rule, (with a few worthy exceptions) mental healers either ignore or jumble together the two interacting and mutually dependant planes, the objective and subjective. To be sure they assert that "all is good," "there is no such thing as evil" "my trust is in the Lord," "the truth shall make you free," etc, etc, ad infinitum, but in ninety-nine cases out of every one hundred they are as blindly ignorant of the *spirit* of the terms they use in this verbal cabala as is the poor Irish peasant when mumbling over his string of beads in an abominably mutilated Latin.

Carefully examine these various statements: "There is no such thing as evil." True, but, if true, then there is no such thing as good. Why? Because we cannot know the one without the knowledge of the other, they are purely relative terms aud can have no existence apart from each other. They are mutual interactions, or polar opposites, when evil ceases to be, good will become equally non-existent.

"All is good." Equally true, but is the real meaning of this statement fully realized? As a rule, no. It is asserted as a mental factor in removing sickness, endeavoring to implant it as a higher thought than the mental distortion which produced the disease, whereas this very sickness is also good, in the strict meaning of this affirmation and its use, both in the abstract and in the objective side of life.

There can be nothing that is not good. The vilest wretch that swelters in the very hotbeds of vice is also good, because he is there. He exists as an objective expression of nature's divine providence or he would not exist at all. He is undergoing a very necessary experience for his peculiar grade of development and is the means of imparting, by example, a valuable experience to more refined natures. Therefore, he is not only good, but is also fulfilling the purposes of Creative life. The assertion that his condition is only an appearance of mortal mind is only true when viewed from that abstract plane of life to which he has not yet attained, therefore such abstract thought cannot apply to him in his present state. In the logic of metaphysics, the premise and conclusion must occupy the same plane, so assuming for the moment the position of mortal mind, we are compelled to say that the most exalted saint and the purest noblest life of man, as typified in the ideal Christ was nothing (so far as earth is concerned) but mortal mind, a mere transitory appearance upon the objective plane of matter. As a fact, both Judas and Christ are equally immortal in degree, the Christ spirit is still in our midst doing its work for humanity, and, we are also surrounded by the spirit of Judas and rampant vice. "As it was yesterday so it is to-day," and will continue so, by comparison, forever.

Once more. "The truth shall make you free." True, O King; Amen. But, what *is* truth? This question is addressed to strictly metaphysical thinkers, and not to those who would answer with some worn out platitude. If the verbal mantrams, the affirmations, and the denials which are given out for the daily use of the weak, the blind, and the sick, have any power, that power must come from an inward realization of the abstract spirit behind the word or verbal expression, *ie.*, from a conscious recognition of the divine idea. To those who have realized the power of this latter statement, the question, "what is truth"? is addressed.

In so far as the studies of the writer entitle him to speak with authority, he can assert as very fact that there are but three expressions to answer the question, viz., I—*I am*, (this he knows). II—*God is*, (all creation asserts this) and III—*Every power and thing in creation is dual and dependent upon every other thing*. This ends the conception of truth, more can only be added from appearance. The vital truths, *I am, God is*, are the alpha and omega; but between these two poles the finite and the infinite, there rays forth all the inconceivable majesty of God's wondrous boundless universe, Creation upon Creation in one incomprehensible vista of fathomless eternities, each particular part of which is a representation of some special phase of nature's divine truth.

The sooner therefore, recognition is taken of apparent truth, upon the plane of conscious knowledge, no matter what plane that may be, the sooner we shall place our lives, our real selves, en rapport with natural law within that degree of life wherein providence has seen fit to place us.

Good and evil, then, are real upon the plane of their expression, and are simply the phenomenal results of harmony and discord, and these are different degrees of vibration. That statement is a *fact* which must be clearly remembered.

Sickness eventuates as the offspring of discord, as do sorrow, misfortune, etc., while *per contra*, health, wealth and happiness are the resultants of harmony. What can be more simple to understand?

The source of disease centers in the fact that the human organism is a medium pure and simple, a complex domain of many diverse kingdoms, a state whose constituent parts are liable to rebellion. The cause, *per se*, of disease is dual, either astro-magnetic or anima-magnetic, the former are the reactions of the stars upon the vibrations of the odylic sphere, the latter, to which the great majority of sickness is due, are the reactions of personal magnetism upon the electro-vital organism.

In the former case, the Sun, Moon and planets, in their progressive motion, form various angles to the radical positions they occupied at birth, when such angles constitute aspects, they produce external results in accordance with their radical nature, if the person's environment offers the necessary conditions for reaction, if not, then they pass away in the embryo state, because the times were not favorable for their manifestation. This is the secret of "arcs of direction" as they are termed.

No arc of influence can possibly operate unless the surrounding conditions are suited

CELESTIAL DYNAMICS.

to its physical expression. When ignorant of this, the latent astro causes, draw man into those very circumstances that evolve the necessary environments for the influences to work out in full. Thus, it is easy to overcome planetary influence by timely knowledge and wise action. The planets urge, predispose and influence, *but they never compel* us to given actions. From full recognition and appreciation of these facts it is easy to know when disease is lurking around us and, forewarned by such knowledge, we can defy it to approach us.

In the latter case, anima-magnetism, we are dependent to a large extent upon our own intuitions, combined with a certain knowledge, that particular temperaments are discordant to us. It is only natural to avoid contact with such. When contrary magnetisms meet they not only clash, as do flint and steel, but they ignite and burn, slowly but imperceptibly consuming the vitality of one or both natures, as the case may be. In some cases where the opposite polarities are perfect, only the negative subject suffers, the positive draws out and consumes the vital forces of the other, until finally death supervenes. Thousands upon thousands of such cases transpire every year, especially among wrongly mated couples. We frequently see persons hearty and healthy before marriage droop and pine away afterwards, vice versa, sickly delicate people revive and get strong. Both cases are the outcome of the same universal law. There is no mortal mind here, but, instead, there is a general tuning up of the physical constitution to the magnetic vibrations of a more intense nature during the conjugal union. Nature is only re-asserting her normal condition that was before latent in the expression of fitful discord. Nothing but universal law prevails, everything is the logical sequence of Divine cause and physical effect.

Self deceive ourselves as we will in the fond hope of power from on high or from within, the vain repetition of meaningless words and stale moss-grown platitudes will never realize it for us.

Vibration alone can so attune our material organism that it shall beat in unison with the higher self and, constant effort until we have struck the key note of ourselves, until our words thrill forth the full power of a quickened Soul is the only sure and certain path to the grand at-one-ment.

The astro-magnetic forces, then, are the primary factors of external life, and vibration is the one grand law of celestial control.

CHAPTER X.

THE DIAGNOSIS OF DISEASE.

That a correct diagnosis of disease is of inestimable advantage to the psychic healer, mental or magnetic, no one can for a moment doubt, but that his diagnosis needs to be the orthodox delineation of modern medical technicality no true student of psychics will attempt to assert. By diagnosis, we do not mean the summary of symptoms classified under some medical term as representative of the disease or diseases thus signified, but we do mean an accurate perception of the radical causes of the physical manifestation of the disease.

Herein, then, we shall differ widely from the modern medical practitioner who has graduated in the schools. To him, a certain array of symptoms mean that the patient is suffering from a certain form of disease, the name of which is very much the outcome of the fashion of the hour. The names of diseases to-day offer a marked and wide contrast to the names for the same afflictions a century ago; "the sore throat" of Queen Elizabeth's day became the influenza of the 18th century, to-day we call it "La Grippe" (whatever that may mean), and almost any form of simple cold and dyspeptic indisposition is attributed to the "Grippe", wherever that name is popular, and as soon as this medical dog has had its day some other equally absurd fad will be introduced as a lay figure upon which mankind can father their thousand and one ailments. Yet in all this time the same laws and the same eternal principals have been in operation and will continue to operate until the very crack of doom. The radical causes of disease have not changed and we will now proceed to lay down a few simple rules by means of which the radical nature and cause of the disease can be ascertained.

But before doing so a few words in explanation seem necessary. It is not absolutely necessary to know the exact hour of a person's birth, (although a valuable thing when obtainable) the day of birth being quite sufficient, and as nearly every one knows the date of their birth there will be very few cases indeed where these rules cannot be applied.

I. Consult an astronomical ephemeris for the day and year of the patient's birth and mark down upon a piece of paper the exact longitude of the Sun, Moon and other planets as given therein, for noon.

II. Examine the position and tabulate the aspects that may exist between the Sun and Moon and the planets.

III. The existing malefic aspects, *ie.*, the evil aspects afflicting the luminaries, indicate the radical source of the patient's disease, and

CELESTIAL DYNAMICS.

the signs which the Sun and Moon and the afflicting planets occupy will correctly show the centers of the constitution from which the sickness proceeds.

IV. If only one luminary is afflicted ignore the position of the other.

V. Count as many days after birth as the patient has completed years of life and take the positions at noon on that day, as at birth, and examine the aspects existing between the two sets of positions.

VI. If evil aspects prevail, as will generally be the case, note the signs from which *the evil* proceeds and you have the secondary factors to complete your diagnosis of the case.

VII. If the evil aspects are separating, and the luminaries are applying to good aspects, recovery will quickly follow with proper treatment. But, if the reverse transpire, prepare yourself for a long fight over a stubborn case.

We will now illustrate these rules in order to show the method of working in actual practice. Mr. X. is seriously ill, cannot leave his bed, etc., etc. He was born April 5th, 1860, hour unknown. By reference to an ephemeris for that date, we find Sun in Aries 15 degrees and 55 minutes, the Moon in Libra 10 degrees and six minutes, Saturn in Leo 19 degrees and 21 minutes, and Jupiter in Cancer 16 degrees and 18 minutes. These being all the factors in the case, we ignore the other aspects. To begin with, the student will here observe that the luminaries are in square to each other showing a discordant interaction between the brain, indicated by Sun in Aries, and the kidneys, as shown by the Moon in Libra. As a fact, the patient was suffering from a severe nervous disorder, melancholia, etc., combined with kidney trouble, but there was also something else that all the medical science in the world would have failed to diagnose, because hidden from sight. Counting thirty days, as the patient was fully thirty years old, which brings us to the 5th day of May, 1860, we tabulate again: Sun in Taurus 15 degrees and ten minutes, Moon in Scorpio 17 degrees and 56 minutes, Saturn in Leo 19 degrees and 42 minutes, Jupiter in Cancer 19 degrees and 49 minutes, while, on this date, we also find the Sun parallel to Saturn. Here we have Sun square Saturn in the birth position, while the Moon is in opposition to the Sun and square to Saturn and this double affliction of Saturn by both luminaries indicates the real secret—*The Heart* shown by Leo—and, upon close inquiry, we found grief and love had been the first cause in the illness. Summarizing, we find the brain and heart are the two points requiring treatment, the recovery from the kidney trouble and sexual derangement, shown by the Moon in Scorpio, will naturally ensue when the primary factors are overcome.

All cases are treated by the same method; the day of twenty-four hours representing one year of life is the cycle of solar motion that rules the life force of man.

There is one exception only to this method of diagnosis, viz., cases of sexual disease, the outcome of personal contagion during coition. And this class of diseases can never be treated successfully from the mental plane alone. This statement will be disputed, but the whole army of mental healers from Mrs. Eddy down to the latest and most accomplished and enthusiastic "scientist," as they are falsely called, are challenged to show a single case of true syphilitic poison that has been cured by purely mental treatment.

It is readily admitted that medicines alone, without faith, are often powerless, but this does not prove the lack of virtue in the medicine. It only proves that medicine, to be really potent, must be taken with conscious faith, this faith arousing into active life the various atoms which compose its active principles and endowing them with the power to attack and ultimately conquer the disease of those parts of the body with which the said atoms have a close astro affinity. So with mental treatment, unless the patient either believes or responds to the thought sent out towards him, the treatment is powerless for good.

It is important to know, next, whether the disease is internal or external, in other words, whether it is the astro-magnetic forces arousing the buried larvae and tainted germs of old racial and hereditary diseases, or whether it is the anima-magnetism of some external organism that the astro powers are making conditions for, ie., the results of personal magnetism, mental and physical. This is very easy to determine. If a feeling of nausea is periodically, or generally felt with the sensation of impending trouble, etc., etc., in the solar plexus, then the sickness comes from some external person or entity and requires corresponding treatment.

Thus the student will perceive that there is nothing at all difficult in this system of diagnosis based upon the celestial dynamic forces of nature. Any person of average intelligence can understand it. Its real beauty and value consists in the fact that it presents a clear scientific system of procedure based upon universal law, while so far no law of any kind has been evolved in the ranks of the mental scientists. Everyone has a way, a whim and a method of his own, consequently cures in every case have been haphazard, not scientific nor commandable. The result of a perfect sympathy in vibration between the patient and healer. Their treatment and prayers did not avail one iota, but their magnetic vibrations did. They never guessed the secret of their real few successes, consequently they could not command the power at will as a scientist ought to do.

CHAPTER XI.

The Treatment of Disease.

We now approach the grand arcana of this branch of Celestial Dynamics, viz., the treatment of disease, and therefore it behoves us to be careful of any misunderstanding upon this very vital subject.

In the first place the student must understand that it is not in accordance with either reason or human experience to suppose that everyone can become a healer. Upon this very subject Saint Paul wisely remarks: "Now concerning spiritual gifts I would not have you ignorant." (I. Cor. XII. 1.)

This is exactly our position. We would not have the student ignorant of the fact that, comparatively, *very few* possess the necessary qualities for successfully practicing "the healing art divine." The spiritual gifts here spoken of are the Soul qualities, as expressed in the magnetic states of the human organism. They are attributes in reality, but gifts by virtue of the fact that the possessor of such, has to render an account of such abilities in the world to come in proportion to his obligations to humanity in this. In the ninth verse of the chapter already quoted, we read "To another faith by the same spirit, to another healing by the same spirit." Faith and healing, you will observe, are twin attributes and are, therefore, mentioned as the compliment of each other. This is as natural in Celestial Dynamics as green and red in art. Those who possess the power always possess the faith, the one cannot exist without the other, they are polar opposites and metaphysically express themselves as *cause and effect.*

The cause of faith is the power *to do*, faith is the effect of the inward ability. But faith and imagination must not be confounded, impressional natures can believe and imagine everything and yet possess no real basis, and to imagine that everyone who studies mental science is capable of healing, is about as absurd as to believe that everyone can become an artist, a musician, a mechanic or a philosopher. And yet, in spite of such a self-evident absurdity, almost the first thing that the "scientist" (?) is requested to do after a preliminary instruction is to "treat." You might as well tell a man who has just learned the names and combinations of the various colors to paint a picture before he had studied the first principles of art, or mastered the elements of drawing, shading, etc., not to mention background, foreground, middle distance, etc., known only to actual artists. We can easily imagine the result. Why not apply this to the metaphysical novice? It is even more to the point than in the case of art. Of course, if real, natural talent be present, the novice may astonish us with an unexpected production in either case, but if, as is most natural, failure is the result, the amateur artist can throw away his disfigured canvas with but little real loss, but the bad work of the mental operator will endure for ages, he has been handling the vital forces of life itself, and the vibrations he has consciously or unconsciously set in motion, are as far reaching as the universe itself, and will continue to bring forth fruit of some sort or other. If that fruit be the distorted reflections of rank ignorance, he has set humanity back so much, he has become a clog upon the wheels of progress and must right the wrong sooner or later. "Verbum Sap."

To be able to treat one's self is, perhaps, within the reach of nearly everyone, that is, everyone of average intelligence and will ability. This is, indeed, a God-send and we ought to be truly thankful for it. To be able to heal others, or rather *capable* of healing others, we require three distinct attributes. 1st, a surplus vitality; 2nd, comparative self control; 3rd, a life generating magnetism. To explain, we require *surplus vitality*, first, the vitality to give without robbing ourselves of the necessary force to react completely from the treatment; second, *self control* to remain unmoved by emotion in the presence of suffering, so as to give forth a calm, steady, magnetic light, a perfect mental picture to the diseased mind that shall be sharp and clear in eveay outline;

(emotion acts upon *the will* like a draught upon the flame of a candle, the whole image is out of focus). Third, *a life generating magnetism* to regalvanize the fading vibrations in the patient, hence the vital force of the healer must be *free* from affliction at birth.

These are the attributes of a healer, possessing these he now requires two qualifications in the patient, or *of him*, viz., 1st, a fair general knowledge of his temperament and disease, and 2nd, an organism that is in direct or indirect sympathy with his own. The first explains itself, the second refers to the astral constitution. They must not antagonize so that, on an average, a duly qualified healer will be able to cure 50 out of every 100 that apply to him. A person *to treat all* will fail in 50 no matter what his qualifications may be, (remember we are now speaking of mental treatment only). Two skilled experts associated together, one born under the fiery trigon, the other under the watery, would be able to treat and cure all cases between them.

In addition to three natural attributes and the two external qualifications, the healer requires the two gifts which come only as the reward of honest labor and research, viz., 1st, knowledge of man; 2nd, common sense to apply such knowledge to the patient's advantage. These are the seven rules, master them all, at least in a great part, before you ever attempt to remove the mote from your brother's eye, lest, in your ignorance, you insert a beam in its place.

Let not the student become dismayed at this array of necessary qualities and conditions. To all those who naturally possess the gift of healing, the training to acquire knowledge becomes a pleasure and success is certain to follow. Just as the artist loves the dry mechanical details of painting, and the musician his laborious lessons and practice, as the necessary grading to their final triumph as master hands, so does the philosophical student, in his patient intellectual work, love all the trials that beset his path as so many stepping stones to perfect wisdom. The medical practitioner gives years of valuable time to the acquirement of knowledge, he has to devote untold hours to hard, dry study before he can honestly obtain his diploma. So it is with the lawyer and the professional expert in every department of human knowledge if success is desired. Wisdom is the outcome of well directed intellectual work, and the mental healer cannot hope for success without the same years of study, physical culture, spiritual unfoldment and psychical research. There is no royal road; there is no secret of success that can be given in a formula or whispered in the ear. All true success is the outcome of well directed patient effort.

You have now the basic foundation to start with, work unceasingly to realize your mental ideal, give your highest thoughts an objective existence.

How to Treat.

This is our next consideration, and we shall pre-suppose that the healer answers to all the necessary conditions and qualifications stated above.

The human brain is the key-board to the musical instrument called man. When this instrument is in tune, all is harmony, there is neither real sorrow nor actual disease. This is a fact, and all treatments based upon the natural law of Celestial Dynamics are conducted upon the principle of vibration exactly as the musician will tune his instrument by relaxing or tightening one or more of the many strings.

The organs of the brain, as classified by phrenology, are the strings or keys to the instrument, and through their medium, in part, can the mental imagery of the mind be reached. There are two methods of treatment, viz., mental and magnetic, both seek the same end, both operate in precisely the same way, and under the same procedure, and the practitioner will frequently find that alternating from the one to the other will produce better results in less time than by either one alone, hence both are recommended.

The system of treatment resolves itself into one of contraction and expansion. The former is cold, contracting and suppressive, the latter is hot, expansive and stimulating. This corresponds exactly to the tightening and relaxing the strings of a musical instrument. In either case, an alteration in the vibration is sought and accomplished.

The functions of the brain externalize themselves in the manifestation of mind, thought and in action. Therefore, everything we can think and every image in the mind, is the outgrowth of some one or some particular group of organs, so that any sickness must have a point of contact in the brain just as every organ in the body is the responsive medium of some group of organs in the brain. Remember these facts.

The spleen is the human galvanic battery whose office it is to store up all surplus force, and also to receive and transmit extra supplies of force when the organism is suffering from depletion. This is one of the most important factors in all the treatments. With these necessary explanations we now come to the actual treatment.

Receive your patient cheerfully and sympathetically. If you find his nature and temperament within the scope of your power, instantly assure him of a prompt and permanent relief. Stand your patient with his back to the light and place yourself a little to the left immediately behind the patient. Then place the left hand upon the region of the spleen. The dress of the patient should be so arranged as to admit the healer's hand to the region of the spleen, which is on the left side below the breast, and energize that organ into intense action, mentally directing your own life current through the left hand to the spleen. While this is going on let the mind be exceedingly calm, positive and *sympathetic*. After about three minutes, never *more than five*, change the polarity of the mind from sympathy to one of lofty, imperious calm, replace the left hand upon the spleen and the right hand upon the brain, with the index finger immediately on the organ or group of organs from which the sickness comes, (if the disease is not functional but purely nervous, "credulity" and correlated organs must be operated upon to remove the *belief* and so destroy the image.) While the hand remains upon the organ formulate a clear, distinct picture of perfect health and freedom to suit the individual case. If the patient suffers from excessive action of the organs, contract their force and reduce the vibrations by the contractive powers of cold, icy, death-like quiet over the organ, if from lack of power of any function, let the treatment be the opposite, viz., hot, stimulating, fiery, active *and glowing with intensity*. This treatment may continue from five to not more than fifteen minutes. After this, let the patient be seated, and immediately in front, back to the healer, then give a general kind of healthy, noble, aspiring treatment, implanting the image of health and strength with an earnest aspiration to awaken the patient's Soul forces to a sense of their powers and duty. Then it is over.

We have described the magnetic treatment. The mental treatment is exactly the same, except that it is purely mental. The healer closes his eyes, enters the silence until he can produce a perfect image of his patient and, when this is done, he mentally performs exactly the same operations without the physical contact. But we recommend the first treatment to be magnetic for the sake of a more perfect rapport.

It is useless to attempt to describe the kind of images to impress upon the brain in different cases. This must be left with the operator. Each individual has his own peculiar conceptions of truth, purity, health and beauty, and these will be more powerful to his mind than the idea of anyone else can possibly be. The great secret rests upon will ability on the part of the healer and faith upon the part of the patient. If these two combine in any perceptible degree, success will follow as naturally as day follows night.

When to Treat.

This is the next important item. The word *when* is used as indicating the commencement of a case and not the subsequent treatments, although even these will have much force. Note these rules.

I. Consult an ephemeris for the current year and note when the Moon forms a benefic aspect with the Sun or planet controlling the disease. Choose that day and time when the aspect is in operation for the treatment, and let the succeeding treatments be given on those days when the Moon, by her motion forms favorable aspects, which transpire every few days. The Moon has wonderful force upon the human brain and, when benefic to the patient, success is much easier.

II. When to refrain from treating. When the Moon applies to evil aspects and, especially so, if she apply to malefic orbs, refrain. Appoint a day when the lunar force is benefic to the rulers of vitality or place of the benefics on the day of birth. Further, if a sinking, sickening or faint feeling is experienced in the Solar Plexus during treatment, immediately stop and appoint another time. If the same occurs for two or three times refuse to treat altogether, as you cannot cure except at the expense of personal suffering, which is not just.

CHAPTER XII.

Man and His Material Destiny, etc., etc.

The true purpose of human embodiment is the acquisition of knowledge through experience, and man's incarnated destiny on earth is the gradual expansion of the forces called and attracted during the past series of impersonal existences; and the precise position, place, and status in society which he may occupy, be it that of the untutored African savage, but little above the brute, or the most cultured representative of modern civilization, is the exact environment that his nature requires for the expression of his incarnated entities.

It is not the outcome of a past karma. It is not the result of previous human incarnation. For man as we know him, never existed on this earth in the human organism before, nor will the same individual ever so exist in the future

The apparent suffering of individuals is necessary discipline or it could not exist. There are no two Souls exactly alike, they can and do exist as counterparts, but their experiences, at least up to a certain point, must of necessity be widely different in degree, and consequently, in effect. Each human being has a certain possibility of Free Will, that is to say a freedom of action and expression absolutely their own, within certain limits, and these limits vary in each individuality. These limits constitute the latitude of the human organism and resemble the latitude of a planet in its orbit about the central Sun. It can wander north or south of its true ecliptic line, but only within certain bounds. Just so man, he can, by the exercise of his own will ability, ascend above the spheres and environments of birth until he reaches the highest point possible to his quality and capacity; or he may sink below such natal conditions until he reaches the lowest point beneath his true central line of life and the distance between these two points, North and South let us say, may be all the real difference externally between vice and virtue, wisdom and ignorance, wealth and want. And yet, notwithstanding their freedom of choice and physical expression in its general outline, as shown in the human orbit from the cradle to the grave, it will be found to correspond in every particular part with the cosmic forces around which the Soul revolves while incarnated amid matter.

Free will, in its limited functions, depends upon capacity, and capacity is the measure of human responsibility, while ability to express being dependant upon environment is the limit of his obligation. This then is the mystery of good and evil, of celestial cause and physical effect.

The great groan of the uninitiated who

feel a strong sympathy for human suffering is, "what is the cause of so much error and pain" "how has this great difference between good and evil become manifest?" The answer is inevitable, simply because nature's end is diversity not equality, because nature needs to utilize every possible expression of his powers upon the earth, both from heaven and hell, in order to round out the God-like being called man. He, the microcosm, born in heaven though dwelling in hell, allied to the Angels, yet possessing all the attributes of the Devil, needs conditions to express and space to fulfil the creative design.

Every Soul requires a certain amount of suffering, no Soul is ever overdosed or gets more than its just requirements, and whether we require this suffering on this, or on the other side of the grave is nature's own secret. She will see that our mission is fulfilled, nor can we escape from prison until, like the debtor of the parable, we have paid our account to the uttermost farthing. Such then is man's material destiny, a rendering of accounts, so to say, of experience and possibility in various realms of impersonal being and a complete expression of each atomic part in the completed organic whole, as we see it so clearly and beautifully expressed in that mysterious temple, the human organism.

Friendly Advice to Students.

We have now completed our course of study in Celestial Dynamics. You will doubtless have observed that, although we have endeavored to be simple in expression, it is one of the mightiest and most sublime of all studies, because it treats of self, of man in his various relations to his fellow man and to God. Be not in any way dismayed at its magnitude. It is easy to learn if you follow this advice. Begin by mastering the primary lessons as taught in our little book, "The Language of the Stars." Commit the rules well to memory; then study in a systematic manner, "The Light of Egypt," which will place you in the second grade and prepare you for this fuller normal course. When you have done this, the present series will be both pleasant to read and easy to fully understand.

In all treatments of disease remember that diseases of contagious virus must be met by the proper medical remedies of a physical nature, in addition to the mental and magnetic method described. This will ensure success. There is no reason for any metaphysician to radically alter his method of treatment. They can each and all gradually combine the two and notice results. What we have especially aimed at is to reduce chaos to order, to bring experiment and haphazard treatment to a clearly defined system of procedure, so that the healer may set to work in a thoroughly systematic manner, and treat scientifically on a natural basis. For, so far, so-called mental science has been woefully deficient in this respect. We have attempted to relegate Mrs. Eddy's mortal mind to the limbo it merits, for if our bodies are mortal mind when viewed from a higher plane, so is that higher plane itself mortal mind when we reach it, viewed from a still higher plane. In fact, mortal mind is as much the mind of God as anything else, all creation in every phase is but the crystalized form of the Deific idea.

Therefore, "read, mark, learn and inwardly digest" these great principles. Our own mission on this plane will soon be completed, and it is our most sincere desire that in leaving the things of earth, we shall at least have been instrumental in making some of its inhabitants wiser and better than we found them. It is the sacred duty of all whose lives have acquired truth to impart that truth to others whenever they are fitted to receive.

Thus we have given our atom which may help to swell the sum total which others already possess.